splashing
through
deep
puddles

splashing through deep puddles

sara salarvand

Edited by Autra Salarvand
Book cover by Francisca Mandiola
Sketches inside by Tien Stencil

Any questions about this book please contact
hello@sarasalarvand.com

ISBN: 978-1-7770808-0-8

a huge thank you to *you* for reading my book
&
thank you to my sister for editing with so
much love. i wouldn't have shared this book if
it weren't for you.
&
thank you to my parents for inspiring me to
do what makes me happy.

contents

this book is about me
and no you don't know me
and maybe it's a bit selfish
to write about myself

i've debated
on whether i should share this
or lock it up

if only you could see
the countless matches i've used
to turn my own dreams into ashes
you would think
i'm no dreamer

between the fire
and the smoke
there was an open path
and i decided to take it

so i sifted the ashes
through my fingers
and let them fall
onto paper
reincarnated
as my own words

maybe it was for me
maybe it was for poetry
whatever it was for
it changed me

so here i am
an open book
each page a piece of me
for you to read

- thank you

part i

the deep puddles
are the ones
you've got to
watch out for

the kind where
your boots
get dirty
your clothes
get wet and

you see yourself
wondering if
you're happy yet

a caterpillar
stuck in
her cocoon

- lost on the inside

as a butterfly
i flutter freely
not stuck
always flying
to anywhere
and nowhere

- lost on the outside too

it's hard
to look at her
straight in the eye
this girl i see
in this puddle

she fidgets and
looks down at
her feet

to look away
from the reflection
which she sees

- self doubt is the enemy

i got lost
following my own tune
the music was unpleasant
so out of discomfort
i will follow you
you seem to know things
better than i do

- pied piper

i just pick at everything
until it falls apart
so maybe then
it'll feel like
everything
is finally in place

- a huge mess

it's not easy
to hold back
the part of you
that hurts

the one that
shows itself
because it needs
attention too

- heal the hurt don't hide it away

winter, you and i can never be friends, can we? i try to let go when you're around but you're just too cold. you don't want me to be happy. you just want my days to be quick and my nights to be long. i hope you can hear me say this through your endless snowfall and roaring winds: winter, i dread you. every year you come back and every time i welcome you with open arms, but you just look away. does my misery bring you pleasure? winter, you prideful fool, you don't know what you're missing. your chill has made me a feeble wreck. things can't possibly get any worse with you or can they? why can't you be more like spring?

i like me
i like me not
i like me
i like me not
i like me
i like me not
i like me

- pulling petals is a full time job

comparison
will be
the death
of me

- and i don't think that it will end there

my defeats erase
all my senses
and sets rage
at the forefront
of my battlefield

- me versus me

my eyes have become the haven for stress
where lashes are picked in torment
where tears gather for each fallen lash
where pain has found home on empty eyelids
where new lashes may bloom
but in fear of being plucked away
they don't flourish into their original ways

here's the thing
i'm happy
then i'm not
i'm happy
then i'm not
i'm happy
then i'm not
and the cycle
repeats

- if you're confused and you know it clap
  your hands

i was afraid to stand out
that's why i didn't try
when i look back now
it's easy to say
i could have been great
when 16 year old me
never thought she was

- self doubt has a home in me

my fears
my doubts
my anxieties
my tears
my outbursts
my rage
my loneliness
my separation
my painful bits

- ingredients for my demons' favourite meal[1]

---

[1] no special measurements needed, the more of each then the tastier it is.

a flower
is still
a flower
even with
all those
missing petals

- i still stand even when i wilt

heart: i want more from life
mind: do you think there's something better?
heart: do you think there can't be?
mind: but aren't you living comfortably?
heart: all i am is comfortably stuck

- to settle or not to settle

every time i reach a peak
my mind thinks
you can do better
but what if all i want
is to enjoy
what i've got now?

- content but conflicted

what a heavy burden it is
to be a 21st century girl
with the pressures of being
what others imagine you to be
their wildest dreams sold to you
and we are let down
over and over
when we cannot conform
with a story that does not fit
the 21st century girl

if your story
happens to pair
with the dreams
we have been sold
from commercials to print
social media to billboard posters
are you satisfied
does your palate agree
with being what they
want you to be?

- taste of reality

i'm a mix of a
sunchild and
moonchild but
i could be a
stormcloudchild
always raising
a bit of trouble
before the rainbow appears

- but where's the pot of gold?

what does it feel like when someone
questions your worth in front of others?

i feel ashamed
ashamed that my heart beats so madly
ashamed that our smiles crossed paths
ashamed that i was good to you
ashamed that your words gave me comfort
ashamed that i let you bring me down
ashamed that i do this to myself every time

- i let you shatter my confidence

there are times
when i think i'm dangerous
untouchable even

you know
the kind of bad girl
you see in movies

a fighter to the end and
nobody can stop me
not man nor god

- will i ever *truly* radiate this vibe?

gimmie a glass of whiskey
i'll drink it all down
sluuuuurmyywoooords
before sundown
i'll tell you a story
of a girl i know
and tell you all her secrets
for hiding is a bore
she'll rise up on to the surface
and once again come alive
but the sad part is
she only wakes
when it's liquor sippin' time

- liquid courage is temporary

i'm swept away
with every step you take
you inspire me
to make my own way
but what if my steps
aren't the same
what if my steps
don't leave any marks
what if my steps
are not as light
what if my steps
are wiped away

- taking the right steps

the most complex puzzle
i've had to piece together
is myself

- still working on it

if you see me
jumping on couches
moving on my tip toes
prancing around
painting dreams on paper
with my watercolor fingers
drifting into my euphoria
please stop me
before i get ahead of myself

- i don't want my dreams to let me down

it's ridiculous how useless i feel on a regular basis. i always tell myself, *it's okay, you just don't have your shit together.* does anyone ever have their shit together? on the surface i may seem patient with life's curveballs being thrown at me, but trust me i'm far from it. if patience was on one side of the football field, then i am on the other.

i constantly fear i am not good enough and that others may think that as well. that feeling of uselessness stems from the part of my mind which is filled with doubt. i cannot tell you the number of times i wake up in the middle of the night telling myself, *do i really have what it takes to do what i want or to do what makes me happy?* my mind replays this doubt over and this nightmare never ends.

part ii

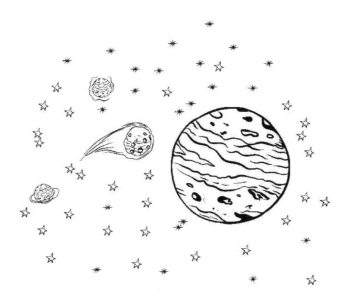

when it kicks in
it scares me
my heart beats fast
my fingers twitch
it takes power over me
and beats me
d
o
w
n
makes me feel small
it knows how to work
its wicked spells on me
a magic trick
on repeat

- anxiety the magician

it's a part of me
a door that will
remain closed

securely locked
the key hidden
a part of me that
will never go away

just like a good friend
who stays by your side
makes sure you're okay

you're stuck with me
to the end
and scaring me
to the point of panic

- anxiety and i

should a meteor hit a planet
the damage is not visible
to the naked eye
but a crater is left in its place
that is what you did to me

- my anxiety's doing

the stars tell me goodnight
and wish me sweet dreams
but my nightmares won't let me
see nice things

i am pushed into darkness
my hands are tied
mouth taped shut
my legs will not move
no matter how much
my deep-sleep-mind
tells them to

it's as if my life
is not tough enough
so my dream fairies think
let's make things harder too

- damn those dream fairies

the keep in my mind
is blocked off
with warnings signs
do not enter
no trespassing
no through road

- i can't seem to go there yet

inhale
you're almost there

exhale
you're almost there

inhale
you're almost there

exhale
you're almost there

inhale
you're almost there

exhale
you're almost there

- separation anxiety

such a mystery
the mind is
her workings are
an enchantment
hexed on the body
to do her bidding

- now if only i could just control it

if you lie for love
does it mean you've done right
or does it mean that love is a lie?

lying is not to be taken lightly
a liar like me would know
it's a pain for the body to carry
hellish for the mind to handle
but mostly disturbing
to have someone give you their trust
in exchange for something made up

you may look at me and think
she has no problems
but i don't wear them
for you to see

my heart is covered
by my sleeves
my mind is hidden
in a sunless corner
and my eyes are closed windows
good at keeping secrets

- concealed

my mind needs a breather
a moment to undress
my worries and sorrows
to be stripped off
so all that is left
is a bare space
for fresh thoughts
but knowing me
i would zip it all up
and continue to feel
overdressed

dear lonely one
doesn't it scare you
that you've spent so much time hiding
because you're afraid of being seen?

oh lonely one
doesn't it worry you
that time is passing you by
and you might miss
taking a chance in your youth?

please lonely one
doesn't it bother you
that you still remain in your shell
when you should have broken it long ago?

- break free already

the candle i hold
drips hot wax
on to my fingers
as i walk through
this dark chamber

my hand
draws across
these rough walls

a moonless abyss
can't stop me
and my dim candle
from finding a way out

- negative to positive state of mind

spring, you always welcome me into your arms unlike that horrible winter. i've never felt lonely with you. the sun you bring is my sweet revival. spring, you help me bloom daisies from madness. i grow tired of waiting for you when winter comes to visit. winter doesn't know me like you do. spring, your temperatures give me balance. i do not hesitate on the scales between love and hate when you are here, but that wretched winter will purposefully tip the scales in its favor and i am too bitter to fight it. spring, could you do one thing for me? when you come back, could you find your way into my heart and stay with me? maybe this time, with you by my side, we can fight winter together.

we speak of it
but why is it
so many still feel alone
in this battle?

we're peeling away at scars
hoping for them to fall off
but those scars are connected
to beating hearts

our pain sits deeper
than the skin
our healing needs to be
from within

- mental health

little monster of mine
come have a sit
talk with me
drink this tea
help me understand
the many riddles
you've set out for me

- one on one

who can i tell my burdens to
when nobody wants to listen?
tell it to the water
the little creature whispers
the water hears everything
your words will move with the river
downstream
the waterfall will carry your tears
and let them pour
crashing into the rocks below
loneliness will be forgotten
so speak to her
for she will listen
and cleanse your tired soul

- nature is your friend

part iii

i had no idea
that some flowers
can survive
throughout every season

- until you picked me

when i was hurting
i did not
hurt others
yet my own friends
treated me
like a puppet
on a string

it took a while
for me to tear
those ties apart
since i had
no scissors

- sometimes you are your only support

there was a pit
of raging fire
i was thrown into
by my
very
own
friends

- school is a nasty place

you chose to look away
from my pleading eyes
and took solace in eyes
which urged you on

- how could you?

nobody wants to know how you feel
they just want to know what happened
and if the story doesn't end how they like
they just move on to the next one
leaving you behind

- it's hard for others to listen to our hearts

in the wild
all species
coexist
knowing that
their survival
relies on
one another
and they
seem to do
just fine

- maybe humans can learn from them too

for once
wouldn't it be great
if and when i say
i'm going to do this
and every single person
responded with
yes, you can

- some don't want you to succeed

there are many who wish
your shoes were empty
so that they could fill it
and tarnish your steps

- some have nothing better to do

be discreet
with your passions
so they are not set loose
for the wind to take hold
passed around to those
who don't want your best

- be careful with who you share your secrets

there is a strangeness in people
i do not understand
they speak of kindness
yet swallow it back whole
the very next day

this hand extended before me
has picked me up
and let me go
many times

it is fear
yet familiarity
which leads me
to reach back
for the very same hands

- these are not the only hands left

i will hold my hand out
for as long as i have to
so that you know
i'm here and
i'm not going anywhere

- never ever

don't throw rocks
at someone who is hurting
throw flowers instead

erase me
go ahead and try
take the white-out
draw a straight line
cause i fall out like
scribbled pen marks
right around the edges
spilling into your dreams
straight from your memories
and you thought it would be
easy to erase me

oh i am so furious
from holding everything inside me
deep down inside me
that even the heavens are now chanting
speak speak speak
but what use is it
when every time i part these lips
i am greeted with spite

- maybe i should stop caring

i was so close
so *very* close
to hating someone
and i swear
i'm not a bad person
but they hurt me
with such a blaze
that not even water
could flush out the pain

but the burns on my body
remind me that hate
only leaves ruins in its place
a fire like that can spread
and leave me scorched for days

i once watched a person
succumb to greed
during a time of weakness

crimson broke out on their face
words ricocheted against walls
pleading hands raised in rage

what a wonderful treasure
for the naivety in me
to see for her own eyes

my epiphany presented itself
their mistake was my saviour
and my time no longer at stake

- i'm putting it in the nicest way possible

i'm not perfect
i have my own faults
but i don't need you
to tell me that
i think my own words
will suffice
for the both of us

- i'm harsh enough

for the sun and i
to shine together
is the most
harmonious pairing
that you and i
could never be

- good riddance

the thorns
on a cactus
may prick me
but at least
i know that
only blood
will drip
from the wound
and that's
the worst
i can expect

- the truth may hurt, but a lie runs deep

some people want to suck
the living life out of you
and when you're a walking corpse
they will be frolicking around
with double the energy
and no care in the world
moving on to their next prey

- i'm old news now

i have sight
but what use is it
if i choose what i see

- open your eyes to what is around you

if trees do not bend
to the whim of the winds
then why should i give in
to the voices of sin

- don't believe them

to all the ones
who entered my life
only to leave it quickly
you each taught me
an important lesson
to stop making
the same damn mistake

- bye bye

i have a heart to give
and i'll place it gently
in my own hands
carefully passing it
on to you
but i worry
you won't hold it
the same way i do

- be careful of who you give your heart to

forget the ocean
you're more like the sea
a mix of blue
a mix of green

a poisonous elixir
masked to be
gin and tonic

a potion i could
sip knowing
it could harm me

a hand so soft
yet so scarred
held out just for me

forget the ocean
forget the sea
you're a mixed up mess
just like me

i never thought the earth
could be so fragile
until you left me that day
she crumbled beneath my feet
i tried so hard
to hold on to her pieces
and she tried so hard
to uplift me
yet in the end we both let go
and laid there in defeat

- hopeless

forget love
i can rebuild that
with someone
new and better but
i've spent precious time on you
and i'll never get that back

- i wish i could

we were together
once upon a time
like a fairytale
all good things
come to an end

good or bad
of that part
i am still unsure

why we started all this
just to let it go
confuses me

you would think
my gut instincts
would have warned me

but my heart
had to get
worked up on you

- heartbreak o'clock

love is like a foreign language
tough in the beginning
too shy to express one's words
each syllable drips from his lips
sweeter than honey
then months pass
we've both learned plenty
a strain to repeat the same words
those sweet syllables
we spoke early on
are now tainted
but you continue
you've come this far
to learn a new tongue
and stopping now
would be pointless
unsure of what to do
so you keep going
until finally
you've learned enough

there was me and then there was you. we
held hands for the longest time, inseparable,
but you chose to let go at one point and
that's when things became a blur. a blur i had
to refocus all on my own.

i don't expect things to go back and
truthfully, i don't want them to. it was only
for a moment when my life had turned gray
and boy was that moment longer than i
thought, but time had my back. time told me,
*"you can get over anything, it won't be easy
and old memories may remain etched in your
heart, but i will heal those scars."*

i always wondered where my happiness ran
off too, but i realize now that i had left it all
with you, i didn't even spare a tiny ounce for
me. so i asked time if my happiness would
return to me. a soft smile grew on time's
face, *"i'll stay here until it does."*

- time heals

it's so cool
how my heart
still beats
on cue
after the many
scars and bruises
you left it with

- the pain you left ain't a thing for me

i close my eyes
searching far and wide
in the garden of my mind
desperate for inspiration and
that's when your heavenly face
comes up
every
damn
time

- and just like that my garden is poisoned

you fan me with flowers
a sweet scented affair
but what happens
when those flowers
are no longer there?

- sweet nothings

the first yellow rose
made me forgive
the second yellow rose
made me forget
the third yellow rose
made me wary
by the tenth yellow rose
i held a bunch of beauty
but it reeked of lost hope

you stung me
a bee in the summer
under the blazing sun
on the way to get some honey
you bumped into me
and for no reason
you stung me

it must have been the flowers
that surrounded me
or the glow of my skin
it could have been
my hazel eyes
mistaken for a honeycomb
or my melancholy voice
that called you in

that bee sting
left its mark on me
but my blood
now runs through you

- hurts, doesn't it?

once upon a time
there was this flower
its pristine beauty
pulled me in

i mistakenly
drank the wine
that dripped
from its petals
when i knew
i shouldn't have

it was unbearable
to place it into the dirt
when it was time
for my flower to go

but i think i always knew
that a flower so perfect
should never
have entered
my home

- i wish you well

i remember you
but barely

it is sad
how my time
once revolved around you
has now gone
but it passed with you too

you are now a distant memory
and it mystifies me
that our seldom greetings
don't mean a thing

and my mind lingers
in those grey areas
the ones you used to fill
with your thoughts

i've moved on
i know that
but i'll never know
when *you* truly moved on
or if you are happy now

i remember you
but barely

any small talk of you
brings a smile to my face
knowing you're fine
makes the void okay

- a love long gone

i pleaded to the skies
to give me what i want
but she said
what is in it for us?
so i asked her what she wants
she shouted
so loud that the earth shook
freedom
freedom
freedom
but i questioned her
from what?

- isn't it obvious?

when will our earth
every living inch
be scattered with
roses not bullets?

when will our earth
get to breathe
a sigh of relief
knowing she can live
without burning alive?

when will our earth
hear sweet lullabies
rather than wake up to
noise from polluted minds?

- when will we give our earth a chance to
  live?

i don't mind
standing outside
under the pouring rain
taking in all the tears

f
  a
    l
      l
        i
          n
            g

from our milky blue sky
lending my shoulder
to my lifelong friend
after all the
food
shelter
warmth
life
she has given me
the least i can do
is be there for her
for as long as she
wants me to be

don't be scared
to let your children
explore life and
explore themselves

what is hidden
from them
does not hide
the fact that
it exists

- just love them, that's all they want

i used to think
i'll stay a star
so close to the moon
within her embrace
but now all i desire
is to be the galaxy
looking over the stars and
encompassing the moon

- thanks mom, i'll take care of you too

just a regular day
on the way to work
my dad was driving
we were talking
as we always do
he responds to something i say
and i cannot recall much else
except this
the only regret i will have
is the day i pass
because i won't be there
to see my daughters anymore

- i was hit with a feeling no words could
  ever express

when i'm stuck in this dark cave
rocks conceal my loneliness
yet your voice will slither
through the tiniest cracks
and help me find a way out

- i can still hear you

i told you i'm broken
i told you i'm a mess
but you whispered
i love you anyway
still it was loud enough
for the clouds to hear
so they shed tears
with me too

if you've drifted away
then you're not a star in my sky
my stars may be few
but they shine bright
and that's enough
to keep my galaxy glowing

- my loved ones

part iv

i was once
told to smile
ohhh
and i did
a sinister smile
not even the devil
can give

he responded in kind
that's much better
but little did he know
that with his words
my insides stirred

i did not smile
for his pleasure
i smiled
for this was only
the start
of my wicked ways

- tell me to smile one more time

i think
you're forgetting
that an item
does not breathe
whereas i do

i'm not something
you can stuff
into your pockets

and take out
to use
whenever you like

- i'm my own person

i love walking
to my car
the bus
the train station
the store
the gym
during the day
but i hate it
at night

- thoughts from a woman

from an early age
a woman is taught
that loneliness
is no proper suitor
and the fear of
being with ourselves
is instilled in us
and in everything we do

- more thoughts from a woman

in chess
the queen can move
vertically
diagonally
horizontally
she has the power
to take out anyone
even the king

since the 15th century
this game has been taught
and played with triumph

yet the real life queens
are powerless
and chess boards
are belittling places
where even the jester
can checkmate her

- even more thoughts from a woman

don't be scared
to talk to a woman
but
you need to be aware
that if and when
a woman says no
then it means <u>no</u>

- repeat after me: no means no

i was once
told to give up
and the one
who uttered
those words
has regretted it
ever since

- i'm a she-wolf

you ever seen
a dragon breathe fire?
well imagine that
but far greater
that's me
yes me

about to burn you down
like a wildfire
and each twig
will lay on the ground
flat and crisp

i watch your fear grow
as my wings expand
now the whole town is dark
your escape is inevitable

you shout at me
weak
stupid
opinionated
b*tch

your words burn
with the touch of my finger
i blow them away
into the pitch-black sky

but don't forget
the words you spit
add fuel to the fire
and will turn me
into the deadliest thing

- dragon's breath

i crawl into a hole
from time to time
to protect myself
from lustful stares
to protect myself
from dirty tongues
to protect myself
from unwanted glares
to protect myself
from a distasteful touch
to prevent things
from happening
because some just can't
help themselves

- some just won't learn

i will not rest
until i become
the very thing
you're afraid of

the very thing
you'll have nightmares of
and wake up
drenched in cold sweat

the very thing
you hear of
day in and day out
and curse yourself

for every time you thought
i would never make it far
for every time you thought
i would never be enough

- mark my words

we harness the same strengths as any man
we possess the same charm
the demons we fight are just as hard
the mountains we climb put us in harm
yet it doesn't stop us from pushing forward

the very doors men have opened
are the same doors slammed in our faces
but we'll break those doors down
to reach the dreams we've been closed off to

thank you to the men who have our backs
thank you to the women who keep fighting
it's time to show the world what we can do

- women and men are equals[2]

---

[2] ex. (women + men) x any race/gender/sexual orientation = human

women
lets be roses
without the thorns
and help other women
f l o u r i s h
from our togetherness

- a bouquet of women

women
don't let them convince you
that you are not good enough
we can break through clouds
toss tornadoes around
and touch the sun
with our bare hands

- she's a goddess

pretty
doesn't even come close
to illustrating her

part v

wake up dreamer
you have been sleeping
for far too long
it is now time
to open your eyes
to the sunrise
and begin again

these wings may have
holes in them
the seasons may have
worn them out
but that cannot
and will not
stop me
from flying

"peace, how are you always so calm?"

i watch you, tediously trying to uncover the answer to your serenity, but i am stuck.

"it's quite simple actually."
"is there a daily ritual or a breathing technique i must do?"
"come sit beside me."
"and then what?"
"hold my hand."
"and what's next?"
"do you see the sun illuminating our blue skies?"
"yes, i do."
"do you see the trees underneath the sun savoring all her energy?"
"yes, i do."
"do you see how she parts those big clouds to wake the land?"
"but peace, i always see these things."
"seeing is only one part my dear, you have to feel it too."

nobody starts life
fully in love
with themselves

we age
so that we
can learn how

i've crossed bridges
only to find myself
stopped at the end
then walking backwards
to the starting point

- some bridges take a long time to catch fire

what will it take
for you to understand
that my life is not
in the palm of your hands

- stop telling me what to do

don't look down my love
the sky is in front of you
and the ground won't get you far

- always look ahead

nasty words
don't belong in your home
for they will rot your walls
bite at your flesh by day
visit your bed by night
and haunt you for life

- i wasn't brought here just to rot

you exceptional human being
your fingers may look soft
but i know
those hands can break glass
and if you bleed
you may weep
but even when it hurts
you'll do it again
because you can

- undeniably strong

i splash
through puddles
some murky
some deep
some shallow
some clean

with each splash
i grow more resilient
with each splash
i continue to change

- growth, is that you?

the flower you thought would never grow
has bloomed far greater than you know

the flower you stepped over and crushed
has been through weather much more harsh

the flower you stopped caring for
well she doesn't need you anymore

- you'll survive with sunshine and rain

i like riding
the waves
any time of day
it doesn't matter
how the current moves
i just keep on
surfing

- playing it cool

let's grow out of our old ways and blossom into the new. i want the sun to look down at us and say, *they deserve our warmth for forever and a day.* i want the moon to beam for us out of the kindness of her heart, for we protected every single star. i want the earth to keep us standing tall, for we did not let her fall. i want the skies to shield us from heavy clouds, for she is bright when we make her proud.

i dug up a grave
for all the words
i was labelled with
all the hurt
i was handed
all the tears
i wasted

but i'm all dry now
dead skin has fallen and
rosy pink sits on my cheeks

you will walk with me
to your grave
you can try your best
to convince me to stay
but you and i both know
it's time for you to go

- 6 feet under part i

i wipe the sweat off my face
all that time and energy
to put *those words*
into a grave
was not as much
as the time and energy
i put into reliving
each haunting memory

with that thought
i look out at the sun
an early bird
just like me
with yesterday
underneath her feet

- 6 feet under part ii

can you believe
i had to put you
into a grave
to get rid of you

i couldn't just let you
bask in the freedom
of our innocent sky
for you would find
your way back to me

your grave is my serenity
the dirt will have you
earth will eat you up
i'm glad you'll never
never ever
see the sun

- 6 feet under part iii

empty dreams
they sit beside me
hands folded nicely
hair tucked behind its ears
their cold presence
graced with carnations
silently awaiting the afterlife
finally
i say under my breath
reality is expecting me

i will no longer have hourglass dreams
no more hiding in secret boxes
filled with bookend fantasies

i will place my dreams outside
so that they can see the sky
fresh air filling their lungs
allowing their hearts to beat with mine

sleepless or not
my dreams will leave my bed with me
to know what it means to be free

- set your dreams loose and see what they
  can do

i cannot choose
between the light
and the dark
they complement each other well
like night and day
like coffee and sugar
you can't have sweet
without the bitter

- how will we recognize the good days
  without the bad?

i don't look at it
as right or wrong
i think of it as
better or worse

- how i make my choices

i tip toe towards my ambitions
you may think i'm just scared
but i'm only learning to walk
side by side with patience
the one thing i've always despised
but never knew i needed

- we're becoming friends

i think there is a fine line between ambition and greed. when is more going to be enough? when have you thought to yourself, *i'm good with what i have now.* i don't ever recall saying that to myself. it's hard to say where i stand, being ambitious is a positive attitude, yet it can turn nasty. it can haunt you. it can change you. it can even maim you. but once you've tasted ambition's treats you just can't go back.

your existence is a wondrous coincidence
hundreds of ancestors leading straight to you
how much more luck does a human need in
this lifetime?

- grateful

the sunrise is my motivation whereas the sunset is my inspiration. the slow dim of the light and the beautiful colors of red, orange, pink, and purple behind the clouds brings this sense of awakening to me. i am bewitched by this beautiful blend in the sky.

the sunset makes me ponder on things i don't think of during the day. i am reminded that i can start anew tomorrow and seeing the sunset with that in mind makes me feel thankful. the darkness can be uplifting, light does not have to be your only muse, but i guess it depends on how you choose to look at it.

earth has accepted us
has given us the right
to walk freely on her grounds
so wouldn't it be wise
to roam around her with love

- she has been so generous to us

the moon looks down at me and asks
*"are you following your dreams like you
said you would?"*
i respond to her with dim-lit eyes
*"i'm sidetracked dear moon, i seem to have
lost sight"*
she then whispers to the stars as they move
closer to her
*"whenever you lose your light, we'll come
together and help you shine"*
i am in awe that anyone would ever do
something so beautiful
something so noble for a nobody like me
when this majestic moon has not once asked
me for a thing

- a selfless act

i'm sorry to myself
for a list of things
but first

i'm sorry
for not listening
to a heart that begs
for me to speak

i'm sorry
for letting others
walk over me
repeatedly

but mostly
i'm sorry
for treating myself
as a single drop
in the ocean

- no more apologies

my condolences to the old me, such a kind-hearted girl. she knew when to speak and when to stay quiet. she knew when to listen which she did mostly all the time. she knew that no meant you are not clever enough to soar sky high. she knew that hiding kept her safe from attention. she knew that a peaceful life meant a quiet one without facing fear.

my deepest sympathies to the old me, she meant well, but her time is up. i have called for her resurrection. this new me, she is a force to be reckoned with. she is now re-born in the very fire that charred her old self to ashes. she is here to live alive. fear can call her by her name but she won't answer. she will be too busy fighting for her peace.

lets make a circle
weaved with lavender and lilacs
candles sitting in a row
we'll hold hands together
share our stories
under the full moon
only the sky can see
our secret sanctuary
where we will howl
where we will wail
where we will feel
together
in our loving circle

i'm not cold blooded
just because i don't want to mingle
i'm not mean
just because i'm honest
i'm not a loser
just because i'm not what you're used to
i'm not ugly
just because i'm not your ideal type of beauty
i'm not stupid
just because i can't answer a question
i'm not foolish
just because i act out
i'm not rude
just because i speak my mind
i'm not cold blooded
just because you say so

i like me
although i'm a pain in the ass
i like me
although i'm not a size two
i like me
although i'm a bit of a pushover
i like me
although i stress too much
i like me
although i've got issues
i like me

- and there's no one else i'd rather be

you don't start
life alone
you don't end
life alone
you are with you
through and through

when my angel's trumpet calls
i don't want any regrets
to be sitting and waiting with me
before my spirit decides to leave

i want to have lived happily
with no worries about the ever after

to have lived peacefully
free as the clouds circling the sky

to have loved infinitely
my heart filled up to the brim with passion

and lastly
to have stood strong by the words
passed down to me by my motherland

- good thoughts, good words, good deeds

are we meant to be happy every single
second of every single day? i don't think so,
at least not always. if we were happy all the
time then what would be the use of having
the ability to feel all those other emotions?
emotions such as anger, fear, and sorrow are
not placeholders. They teach you strength,
resilience, patience, and most of all love. our
emotions are what give our passions
meaning. happiness is not the only emotion
which pushes you into becoming a better
person.

we shouldn't get ourselves swept away in
anger or sorrow, that's not ideal nor healthy,
but we can grow from it and even nurture
these emotions so that our bodies do not
remain in fury. happiness is something we all
want and deserve, but don't beat yourself up
if you don't feel it every single day.

- happiness, the journey

love is the centerpiece of life
without it i would never know
how to leave pain behind

it is love which i find in soft eyes and in open hearts. it is love where i find a helping hand in a person i have never met and may possibly never meet again. it is love that creates imperishable bonds that turn us into eternally binding souls. it is love that makes us fight ceaselessly for all the right reasons. it is love that does not look for our differences and sees humanity as one. it is love that helps us breathe easy and mends all our grief. and in the infinity of love lies our reason for living with a purpose.

- the answer is love

believe in this world
for it has plenty soft spots
where love still pours from

believe in this world
for it will shower you with kindness
even when you are at your lowest

believe in this world
for the earth is made of magic
there for you when you least expect it

precious dance
take me in
i want to feel every step
the rhythm on my skin
my beating heart
will follow the tune
this alluring music
unravels my every move
i will dance
this precious dance
and forget you

oh great seeker of beauty
they don't understand you
because their hearts are closed off
and their eyes can't dig deep

you are beauty
so skin deep
that if they cut you
flowers would bleed

- a beauty unseen

cherry blossoms
aren't meant to be picked at
they should stay
where they are supposed to be
blooming on your skin

- pimples

i love it when i'm happy
what a ridiculously
beautiful emotion

it makes you feel so
whole
and unlike anger
which feeds off of you
leaving you empty
a bottomless pit

happiness feeds your body
with vitamins and minerals
money can't buy

- priceless

what does real beauty look like
when you're so happy that
you don't give a f*ck
what you look like
on the outside
and if someone says to you

did you gain weight
stop eating
what's wrong with your skin
your butt is too big
no more piercings
thunder thighs
don't cut your hair
your butt is too small
tattoos aren't for girls
you're so skinny

well the joke is on them
those words used to hurt
now i just walk away
laughing
as their words
float in the air
with no one
to cling to

life is my story
i write it as i go
tangled with the tales
of friends and foes
scribbles we wrote
on pages unknown
some had chapters
i'd rather keep closed
some pages were open
for my eyes to soak
my own story
may never be well known
but i'm grateful i can share
my heart's words on paper
a narrative about a woman
who wants happiness
to become her home

- not the end

why do i run into darkness so willingly? if i'm so useless then how am i still here? why do i have to question every little thing i do? i am tired of placing weight on to self-doubting thoughts. i am ready to feast on positivity for as long as i am able. luck has brought me here, but my strength is what keeps me going.

don't let them clip away
at the wings you've grown
out of pain and love

their single snip
is not worth it
you've got too much
to fly for

since you have taken a chance on me and
have read about my dreams and worries, i
want you to take a chance on yourself.

don't pick at yourself, don't sweep your
insecurities or fears under the rug. you
deserve to be seen and heard. so go on and
take a look at yourself in the mirror and don't
shy away. enjoy the parts of you which you
love, but don't allow your flaws to feel
unwanted.

put those flaws on a pedestal and let them
shine. go outside and let the sun bring them
to light. don't be afraid, go on. that ethereal
beauty you see in your wildest fantasies, that
is you. i'm telling you, that ethereal beauty is
you as you are now.

i'm slowly
turning into
my very own
dream come true

to love yourself
it is a slow love
starting with the roots
one that goes through the seasons
one that may wilt from time to time
but you will blossom if you care for each
petal
you will bloom out of the dark days and
into a colorful bouquet
even with the small holes etched onto the
leaves
you will still shimmer under the sun
you will still glisten under the moon
slowly starting to understand how
to love yourself

- the greatest love story

my universe has shifted
ever since i decided
to be me
unapologetically

no more wincing at mirrors
no more hiding behind doors
no more inhales without exhales
no more giving in to others
no more giving in to myself
no more waiting for the right moment
no more impatience with patience
no more dreams without action
no more action without dreams
no more tears when cruelty knocks
no more listening to pessimism
no more anger sitting in my bones
no more letting fear go after my heart
no more escaping the deepest of puddles
this time i'll be splashing through them

Made in the USA
Middletown, DE
16 May 2020